Walking Humbly

Scripture Meditations in Verse

THOMAS FLOWERS

Grace and peace to you,

Thomas Flowers, SJ

Paulist Press
New York/Mahwah, NJ

Cover design by Sharyn Banks
Book design by Lynn Else

Library of Congress Cataloging-in-Publication Data

Flowers, Thomas.
    Walking humbly : Scripture meditations in verse / Thomas Flowers.
        p. cm.
    ISBN 978-0-8091-4571-3 (alk. paper)
    1. Bible. N.T.—Devotional literature. 2. Bible. N.T.—Meditations.
I. Title.
    BS2341.55.F66 2009
    242'.5—dc22

                                                    2008033712

Published by Paulist Press
997 Macarthur Boulevard
Mahwah, New Jersey 07430

www.paulistpress.com

Printed and bound in the
United States of America

Contents

Preface v

PART ONE:

Disciples 1

PART TWO:

Encounters 39

Preface

The incarnation offers a challenge to our imagination: How are we, as Christians, to fathom Jesus, who is at once a human like us, and is also God, awesome and majestic? The notion of Jesus as human is, perhaps, the more difficult one, made no simpler by the way in which scripture (the clearest key to the *person* of Jesus) can seem so cold and distant. This book is intended to provide a way for you to draw closer to the person of Jesus and other familiar figures in the Bible.

What you will find on the following pages is a series of scripture passages, followed by poetic reflections and reflection questions. The poems are meditations upon the scriptures with which they are paired, and offer a perspective on the people and events of the passages that is not necessarily part of our normal reaction to these mostly familiar biblical accounts. They represent the fruit of my own reflection and imagination, but are meant to open a door for you to enter into your own meditation. This is why there is a reflection question after each poem, for it is my sincere hope that my poems will enable you to think about the scripture in a new way. The questions, indeed, are often very close to what I asked myself before sitting down to write the poems. Your answers may be very different from mine, but that will only give you the benefit of yet another way of looking at the same passage.

The first section, *Disciples,* consists of scripture and reflections on particular people from the Bible. The second section, *Encounters,* deals more specifically with the person of Jesus, taking events in the scriptures and bringing them into our daily lives as Christians. The entire book is about our relationship with the Lord. It is intended to enhance your own prayer, your own reading of scripture, and your own ability to apply the teachings of scripture to your life. You will find that the poems are very accessible, even if the meaning of the scripture texts does not at first appear to be obvious. It is for this reason that this book is not so much meant to be read straight through as to be prayed and lingered over—for in the accessibility of the poems and in your own answers to the reflection questions, perhaps the scriptures will open to you as never before.

PART ONE

Disciples

1 Samuel 3:8–10

THE LORD called Samuel again, a third time. And he got up and went to Eli, and said, "Here I am, for you called me." Then Eli perceived that the LORD was calling the boy. Therefore Eli said to Samuel, "Go, lie down; and if he calls you, you shall say, 'Speak, LORD, for your servant is listening.'" So Samuel went and lay down in his place. Now the LORD came and stood there, calling as before, "Samuel! Samuel!" And Samuel said, "Speak, for your servant is listening."

Upon Being Awoken

Sometimes it's hard to answer the phone
In the middle of the night.
For one thing, I usually don't know
What that ringing is.
And when I figure it out on some late ring,
It's hard to find the phone.

But I've been called out of sleep before
And today it makes me think of Samuel,
Though it's hard to believe that voice
On the other end of the phone
Belongs to the Lord.

Sometimes life isn't very subtle,
Which is convenient for the stubborn
Like me.

So speak. I'm listening.

For Reflection: *Recall a time when you had trouble recognizing the voice of the Lord. Did the Lord eventually "get through" to you? How?*

Jeremiah 20:7–9

O LORD, you have enticed me,
    and I was enticed;
you have overpowered me,
    and you have prevailed.
I have become a laughing-stock all day long;
    everyone mocks me.
For whenever I speak, I must cry out,
    I must shout, "Violence and destruction!"
For the word of the LORD has become for me
    a reproach and derision all day long.

If I say, "I will not mention him,
    or speak any more in his name,"
then within me there is something like a burning fire
    shut up in my bones;
I am weary with holding it in,
    and I cannot.

A *Fire Burning*

My feet hurt
Putting on Jeremiah's shoes,
My eyelids drooped with weariness
Looking through Jeremiah's eyes,
My thoughts were heavy
Carrying Jeremiah's burden,

But I knew
Like Jeremiah knew
That there was a fire burning.

And though not every word
Promised sweetness, promised happiness,
I knew they were your words,
My words to hear and speak,

And they were my relief,
The only joy worth having,
Though I tried to escape,
Though the night was dark with curses.

It was you, Lord, who promised,
Who denied the impossibility,
Who saw beyond our feeble sight,

And when the light
Dawned on the darkness
Of the empty tomb that day,
When Jesus—
Who died much like Jeremiah—
Was raised from the dead,

I saw it with Jeremiah's eyes,
Your fire burning,
Your word, your life
Filling up my weary spirit
With irrepressible light.

For Reflection: *Have you ever experienced Jeremiah's reluctance to speak the truth? Compose a prayer asking for Jeremiah's help at such times.*

Matthew 1:18–20

NOW THE birth of Jesus the Messiah took place in this way. When his mother Mary had been engaged to Joseph, but before they lived together, she was found to be with child from the Holy Spirit. Her husband Joseph, being a righteous man and unwilling to expose her to public disgrace, planned to dismiss her quietly. But just when he had resolved to do this, an angel of the Lord appeared to him in a dream and said, "Joseph, son of David, do not be afraid to take Mary as your wife, for the child conceived in her is from the Holy Spirit."

Matthew 7:24–25

[JESUS SAID:] "Everyone then who hears these words of mine and acts on them will be like a wise man who built his house on rock. The rain fell, the floods came, and the winds blew and beat on that house, but it did not fall, because it had been founded on rock."

Into Your Home

I wonder if
When he talked of foundations,
Splinters, beams,
Cornerstones,
It always made him think
Of the carpenter who taught him
About such things,
Of you,

And your calloused hands showing him
With what work building kingdoms began.
Because without you,
There was no beginning,
No home for him
Who would have seemed
An illegitimate child to a too young mother
Without you,

Without you,
No doubt full of dread and misgivings,
Wondering and fearing,
But loving the Lord and his mother,
Making them a home
The only way you knew how to,

And I wonder today,
Feeling unworthy of working
To build his kingdom,
How unworthy you felt

To be the one teaching him,
Receiving his kiss,
Being called father
When you weren't,

And knowing,
When he spoke of his father
And the kingdom they were building,
That you were there,
In the foundation.

For Reflection: *Recall someone who has helped you build the foundation of your life with Christ. How did this person do this? Compose a prayer of gratitude for this person.*

Mark 1:9–11

IN THOSE days Jesus came from Nazareth of Galilee and was baptized by John in the Jordan. And just as he was coming up out of the water, he saw the heavens torn apart and the Spirit descending like a dove on him. And a voice came from heaven, "You are my Son, the Beloved; with you I am well pleased."

John the Baptizer

I sat on a rock this afternoon,
Trying to gather back my thoughts,
Wondering where they all went,
And imagining that John the Baptist
Sat beside me on the shore.

And there we were, weary
In the familiar wilderness
With plenty of crooked paths
That needed straightening,
And the sound of John's voice,
Now two thousand years old,
Still echoing around us.

And I wondered aloud if he was sad
To see his disciples leave
And follow someone else,
Or if his voice was hoarse from shouting
And not being heard,
Or if there wasn't just a pang of regret
When the heavens opened up
And he knew for sure
That it wasn't him God had chosen.

He just looked at me in response,
With the weariness of the wilderness
Showing all about him
And a fire still caught in his eyes,
A passion still burning
For crooked ways made straight.

And I realized, for the thousandth time,
That it was never going to be me
For whom the crooked ways became straight
And that it wasn't my love that made John hoarse.

But I left the ghost of the Baptist
With a fire caught in my eyes—
Baptized by his love.

For Reflection: *Recall a time when you had to humble yourself for the sake of the Lord. How did you grow through this experience?*

John 2:1–5

ON THE third day there was a wedding in Cana of Galilee, and the mother of Jesus was there. Jesus and his disciples had also been invited to the wedding. When the wine gave out, the mother of Jesus said to him, "They have no wine." And Jesus said to her, "Woman, what concern is that to you and to me? My hour has not yet come." His mother said to the servants, "Do whatever he tells you."

That Much You Knew

My mother won't bother
With my protestations either.
Not when she knows.

And so you did
The meek, humble, womanly thing—
You told Jesus what to do
When he didn't want to do anything,
And he listened, despite how it sounded,
Despite how he must have felt following you

When you didn't really know
What it meant to nudge him forward
Or what he'd do.

Because it wasn't just water to wine,
It was hearts of stone
Melted into flesh at his word,
It was life that he'd give
And give back
When his hour had come.

But he wasn't
Just your son,
That much you knew,
So you told him to go,
Though you didn't know

He'd go to be broken,
To die
Before you.

No, I don't think you knew,
But sometimes being a mother
Is knowing when you don't
And saying, "yes, go,"
Even when you do know.

For Reflection: *Recall a time when you acted in faith without knowing what the outcome would be.*

John 3:1–3

NOW THERE was a Pharisee named Nicodemus, a leader of the Jews. He came to Jesus by night and said to him, "Rabbi, we know that you are a teacher who has come from God; for no one can do these signs that you do apart from the presence of God." Jesus answered him, "Very truly, I tell you, no one can see the kingdom of God without being born from above."

Nicodemus

Was it that you couldn't sleep?
Couldn't turn to dreaming
One more night,
One more time
To tell yourself
Everything was going to be all right?

And then fear
Was darker than the darkness
And you weren't sure
If you were more afraid someone would see you
    on the way
Or that you'd make it undetected
And he'd answer when you knocked.

Was it something you always knew?
Something wrong inside you,
Seemingly incurable, and aching
To find a remedy,
To find the light
You saw glinting in his eyes?

And then the tears
Came unbidden like the longing
You no longer knew how to contain,
And all you wanted was his "yes,"
His lips to say
There was hope for a broken soul.

Was it a restless contentment?
Restless in how you sought
To be content like you were
When he smiled,
When he opened your eyes
To what love was?

Because if that was it,
I understand.

For Reflection: *What keeps you restlessly seeking God?*
What gives you contentment?

Luke 6:12–16

NOW DURING those days he went out to the mountain to pray; and he spent the night in prayer to God. And when day came, he called his disciples and chose twelve of them, whom he also named apostles: Simon, whom he named Peter, and his brother Andrew, and James, and John, and Philip, and Bartholomew, and Matthew, and Thomas, and James son of Alphaeus, and Simon, who was called the Zealot, and Judas son of James, and Judas Iscariot, who became a traitor.

Twelve

Perhaps
Andrew was used to Philip's tricks,
And James always knew what Peter's half a smile meant.
Or Thomas liked to wake up at three
Just to stare at the morning stars for a moment,
And always disturbed Jude
When he got up,
Who liked to tell the same old jokes
Whenever a new ear or two might have
Been around,
But somehow always did so
When John was nearby, too.

I've known companions
And as briefly as I've been on this road,
It's been awhile
And enough not to know
What some people are doing in my life,
And to long for others to stay
Just a bit longer than they do.

I've known idiosyncrasies
And faults and charms
And the seemingly insignificant way
A certain someone cuts his food.

And I think they knew, too,
That night in what couldn't have been
More familiar company,
Or anywhere less
Than where their hearts wanted to be.

And maybe James
Was annoyed with Bartholomew,
And Judas and Simon
Had had a pleasant talk together that day.
And Matthew had walked beside Jesus
In silence for a long time.

And they were just friends
And longtime companions,
Dreading the end he kept talking about,
And scared to think
What all he did and said that night meant,

With the air thick with meaning
And foreboding.

Twelve companions—
Who could have just as soon
Been friends of mine—
Unaware what a few companions
Would do to the world.

For Reflection: *Who are your companions in spreading the good news? What are they like? How do you help one another in being Christ for others?*

Matthew 9:9

AS JESUS was walking along, he saw a man called Matthew sitting at the tax booth; and he said to him, "Follow me." And he got up and followed him.

Called Foolish

I'm sure he knew
That some would say
They both were fools:

He a fool for abandoning the comfort
He'd so carefully built,
And Jesus a fool for trusting
A conniving swindler like Matthew.

But that day
With the sun in his eyes,
With the dust in his skin,
He must have been waiting,
Though for what, I doubt he knew

Until the fool was standing
In front of Matthew's booth,
Cheap clothes, rough hands,
Smile infectious, irresistible.

And as the words came
To Matthew's ears,
They were all he longed to hear,
And so he walked away
From his foolish pursuits
After the fool who asked him
To follow.

I'm sure he knew
Then that he was a fool
Who'd been fooling himself
For most of a life,
Who didn't mind being a fool
If he was Christ's.

Mark 10:35–37

JAMES AND JOHN, the sons of Zebedee, came forward to him and said to him, "Teacher, we want you to do for us whatever we ask of you." And he said to them, "What is it you want me to do for you?" And they said to him, "Grant us to sit, one at your right hand and one at your left, in your glory."

Brothers' Love

Maybe they were seeking glory
When they asked to be
At his right hand and his left,
Different, maybe better, than the rest.

But I watched them on the first day,
Before everything in their lives changed,
When they were just mending nets,
Serving the Lord, and serving their father,
The only way they knew how.

And I've noticed that it's James and John—
Nearly inseparable: one follows the other,
Time after time when we hear of the brothers,
The sons of Zebedee.

Maybe I'm seeking glory too,
And like them, I'll be rebuked
As many times as I need to be.

But they must have been in that boat,
Cowering with the others that night,
As he came across the waves,
Wearing his power and his glory modestly
And making them worry
And wonder what this was.

And maybe they were seeking glory,
Just like so many of us are,
But he didn't tell them to leave,
And though they undoubtedly didn't get
Their chosen seats by the Son of God,
The King of Kings,
The Judge of Judges,
In all his glory,

If they had, I don't think
There would have been James on the right
Without John on the left.

Whatever else they whisper to us across the ages,
That's something powerful and glorious
About brothers' love,
Which is, at least, a good place to start.

For Reflection: *Recall a relationship in your life that has led you to a deeper understanding of God's plan for you. What is unique about that relationship?*

John 14:8–9

PHILIP SAID to him, "Lord, show us the Father, and we will be satisfied." Jesus said to him, "Have I been with you all this time, Philip, and you still do not know me? Whoever has seen me has seen the Father. How can you say, 'Show us the Father'?"

Philip's Friend

I can see it in my mind:
My little room, a cozy-looking bed,
A sweet melody in the air,

And a bookshelf with all those things
I kept meaning to read,
And now have time to,
And room for sitting and talking and laughing
With all those people I love,
Who are bound to stop by:
A comfortable resting place—
As much like a room in heaven,
As I can manage to imagine at the moment.

But Philip said what I'm thinking:
He may have patiently explained,
For perhaps the thousandth time,
That he was the way and the truth and the life,
And that all we needed to do,
Was believe and follow—keep on following,
Just like we had been doing.

But Philip spoke as I sometimes feel:
Just show us,
Tell us who God is,
Tell us why we should believe
That there are rooms in heaven
Carved out for us,
When we know of the cavernous depths of our souls
Where we carve out refuges
For sins and doubts and failings.

Tell us who this is
Who could make such a promise
To us.

To me. And Philip.
Who believe
But just don't get it.

For Reflection: *What do you "not get" about your faith in Christ? Compose a prayer to the apostle Philip to help you.*

Luke 10:40–42

BUT MARTHA was distracted by her many tasks; so she came to him and asked, "Lord, do you not care that my sister has left me to do all the work by myself? Tell her then to help me." But the Lord answered her, "Martha, Martha, you are worried and distracted by many things; there is need of only one thing. Mary has chosen the better part, which will not be taken away from her."

John 11:39–40

JESUS SAID, "Take away the stone." Martha, the sister of the dead man, said to him, "Lord, already there is a stench because he has been dead for four days." Jesus said to her, "Did I not tell you that if you believed, you would see the glory of God?"

Along with Martha

With saucepans and spice,
Flour and pie tins
Passing rapidly though our hands,
We'll ask, in our defense,
What's wrong with the kitchen,
Where's the sin in working tirelessly
To make an evening or a day
Perfect for everyone else?

Martha was only making sure
The food wasn't overcooked
For the savior of the world.

And it was Martha who believed
That Lazarus would come back
This day or the last
If that's what Jesus said,

But doubted enough
To worry about the stench,

And it's Martha,
Of confidence and practicality,
Who makes us so afraid,
So accurate a picture
Of our heart's condition—
Worried over many things
And complaining that everyone else
Isn't worried enough.

But I like to think that Martha
Wasn't so anxious she missed
What I usually do in my anxiousness:

He didn't say to stop
Being a wonderful hostess,
He said to stop worrying
Over what Mary was doing,
He said to stop worrying
Over what Martha was doing.

And maybe that night
Washing dishes
Became Martha's prayer.

For Reflection: *What aspects of your work for God can you make into a prayer? How can you do this?*

Luke 6:13, 15

AND WHEN day came, he called his disciples and chose twelve of them, whom he also named apostles.... Simon, who was called the Zealot.

Simon

I wonder what Simon thought
When it came time for Jesus
To wash his feet,

For he who was called a zealot
Was not Peter protesting
And loudly demanding,
Nor John resting his head
Against his rabbi's chest,
Not Judas departing,
Not bold Thomas,

Just Simon numbered, named,
And quickly forgotten.

I like to think,
Feeling inconsequential
These days,
That it was enough

To be there,
To listen and not leave
That evening,
As on so many before,
Doubting and failing,
But remaining

The one Jesus chose,
And chose once more that night,
Cold water and his touch
Sending shivers up Simon's skin,

Simon satisfied to be lost
To history, to fame,
But named
A friend of Jesus.

For Reflection: *Whom do you know like Simon, a friend of Jesus but without much public credit? What about this person makes you regard them as a friend of Jesus?*

John 19:38

AFTER THESE things, Joseph of Arimathea, who was a disciple of Jesus, though a secret one because of his fear of the Jews, asked Pilate to let him take away the body of Jesus. Pilate gave him permission; so he came and removed his body.

Kingdom Come

Because I wasn't there,
I can only weep at the sight someone else described,
And I can only imagine the smallest bit
Of the agony he felt as he died,
And the despair in their hearts,
As they watched from the foot of the cross.

There were a lot of people
Who weren't there that day,
And knew, in their hearts, that they should have been.
And that day, Joseph, from Arimathea,
Certainly wasn't there to watch him die,
But he had hardly been there to watch him live,
And so I suppose that made sense.

But not to him, I don't think.
Because maybe being a secret follower,
Had been all right, while he was alive,
While there was time for earthly affairs,

But the moan of the earth,
As he breathed his last breath,
Must have been nothing compared
To the splitting open of Joseph's soul,
As he realized that it was too late for him,
That his kingdom had already come,
That his treasure was stored up
In the earthly pleasures around him,
And there was nothing waiting for him.

And so what did it matter anymore,
This hiding—he approached Pilate in daylight,
And used his treasure and his power
To give Jesus's body a place of comfort.
If wealth was good for anything,
He could at least do that much,
Too late as it was.

And when he found, a few days later,
That his tomb was empty once again,
I think he realized something easy enough to miss:
That too late, isn't, and despite what he had thought,
It was only with an empty tomb
That he could see the kingdom coming.

For Reflection: *What "earthly things" hinder you from experiencing Christ fully? How can you ask Jesus for help in overcoming these hindrances?*

Luke 8:1–2

SOON AFTERWARDS [Jesus] went on through cities and villages, proclaiming and bringing the good news of the kingdom of God. The twelve were with him, as well as some women who had been cured of evil spirits and infirmities: Mary, called Magdalene, from whom seven demons had gone out....

John 20:15–16

JESUS SAID to her, "Woman, why are you weeping? For whom are you looking?" Supposing him to be the gardener, she said to him, "Sir, if you have carried him away, tell me where you have laid him, and I will take him away." Jesus said to her, "Mary!" She turned and said to him in Hebrew, "Rabbouni!" (which means Teacher).

Her Name

There's a lot I don't know
About courage.
I think I would have been hiding with the rest,
Or alone, crying.

She was crying too,
Just three days after he died,
As she came to the tomb
To tend to the only needs of his
There were left to tend to.
And when she found him gone
It was too much,
And all she wanted to do
Was to find him,
And cling to what was left
Of her life.

She must have heard him
Say it so many times,
And maybe it always made
Her think of the first time
He had spoken her name,
And driven out the demons,
When he had saved her
And changed everything.

So maybe the others could hide,
But she had to be near him,
She had to care for him even if it was too late.

And then she heard, "*Mary*,"
Her name, in his voice,
And it was unmistakable,
And it wasn't too late:
His voice could still calm storms
And shatter hearts of stone
And cast out every demon
Of fear and loneliness, from her heart.

She heard him say her name that day
And had the courage
To let him change her life again.

For Reflection: *How would you respond if Jesus called you by name? How might such an intimate call change your life?*

John 21:3–4

SIMON PETER said to them, "I am going fishing." They said to him, "We will go with you." They went out and got into the boat, but that night they caught nothing. Just after daybreak, Jesus stood on the beach; but the disciples did not know that it was Jesus.

Fishermen

Sometimes I think
We all get the feeling
We should just go back to fishing,
Just move through the familiar ways,
Just pick up where we were
Before everything got so complicated.

But there weren't fish that day,
And even if there had been
Everybody was looking at him
From the corners of their eyes,
Waiting, as if Peter knew what to do,
As if he weren't just a coward.

And there weren't fish that day,
Until he was standing on the shore
Calling to Peter,
And then it didn't really matter,
Except that Jesus wanted fish for breakfast
And Peter had fish to offer.

And maybe
A love that hadn't been enough
To contend with fear
When the world had gotten dark,
Wasn't enough.
Maybe he'd see through
Every sincere profession
To the weakness.

But seeing him again,
Peter knew
That he couldn't go back to fishing.
And when he was asked to follow,
His fearful heart
Didn't hesitate.

For Reflection: *When have you wanted to "go back to fishing"? What turned you back from your "security zone" to embracing Jesus?*

John 11:16

SO THOMAS, who was called the Twin, said to his fellow disciples, "Let us also go, that we may die with him."

John 20:24–25

BUT THOMAS (who was called the Twin), one of the twelve, was not with them when Jesus came. So the other disciples told him, "We have seen the Lord." But he said to them, "Unless I see the mark of the nails

in his hands, and put my finger in the mark of the nails
and my hand in his side, I will not believe."

Doubting Thomas

This is, after all, what I do.
I wouldn't have walked on water, like Peter,
Which I guess means I probably shouldn't fall.
And I wouldn't have been there at the very end,
    like John,
Nor would I have been Mary at the tomb that day.
And I wasn't a tax collector in some other life.

But I have a love like Thomas's,
Who wanted to go to Jerusalem and die,
If that's what was being asked of them,
And who wasn't there when Jesus came back,
Perhaps because he was sick, like they say,
But may have, I think, needed some time alone
To weep in hopelessness
As he watched the pieces of his broken heart,
So long ago surrendered,
Slip silently through his fingers.

I know why he didn't believe then,
Especially on nights like this
With the cold coating my skin
And with my weary mind tired of trying

And with the loneliness of love
For company.

And Thomas, forever in our minds,
In doubt,
Needed to feel with his hands
The pain this man,
Who had died instead of him,
Had endured.

And Thomas recognized,
For the first time, his Lord,
On the other side of pain:
Somewhere in faith

With his doubts and the loneliness of love
Now his second-best companions.

For Reflection: *Recall a time when what God offered seemed "too good to be true." What made it seem too good to be true? Ask for Thomas's help to overcome these obstacles.*

PART TWO

Encounters

Philippians 2:5–7

LET THE same mind be in you
    that was in Christ Jesus,
who, though he was in the form of God,
   did not regard equality with God
   as something to be exploited,
but emptied himself,
   taking the form of a slave,
   being born in human likeness.
And being found in human form....

In Flesh

And though the habits of
My self-destructive teeth,
And a digestive tract
Laced with booby traps,

Seem almost alone enough
To make yours a foolish will,
They only signal the beginning
Of our life in this flesh,

With the weight of ancestry
And the accumulation of sin,
With the burden of anxiety
And the brittleness of nerves,

But still you came that day
Knowing as we couldn't
All that we'd done to twist
These earthly frames.

And you came not despite
Our fear and endless doubt,
Not regardless of the pain,
Not ignoring the carnality,

But rather because of it,
Rather because you meant it
When you said so long ago
That you were God with us.

For Reflection: *What about your life in the flesh do you have the hardest time inviting Christ to share?*

Luke 19:5–6

WHEN JESUS came to the place, he looked up and said to him, "Zacchaeus, hurry and come down; for I must stay at your house today." So he hurried down and was happy to welcome him.

His Eyes

I wonder if I could see
The tumultuous waves,
Rushing stormy into quiet
In his eyes,

Or if they'd be
Brown as loaves
Pulled from the oven,
Green as grape vines
Fruitful in springtime,
Bright as lightning,

Or if I could stand the sight,
Staring at them across a table,
Long after the meal,
Seeing my reflection
Unworthily caught in
Their luminous depths,

Or if I've seen them:
Like on the first day
When he could have looked
Anywhere but didn't,
When he looked at me,
As if my poor appearance
Were enough to lift away the cares
Of his weathered expression,

And with kindness pooled
In his eyes to match
The tears appearing in mine,
He asked me if I would please
Come along and help him.

For Reflection: *What would you hope to see, looking into the eyes of Jesus? What would you be afraid you might see?*

Matthew 4:1–3

THEN JESUS was led up by the Spirit into the wilderness to be tempted by the devil. He fasted for forty days and forty nights, and afterwards he was famished. The tempter came and said to him, "If you are the Son of God, command these stones to become loaves of bread."

Desert Revelations

It's so easy to think it was easy
For the Son of God to act that way,
Easy to assume there was no doubt,
No subtle hesitations lurking
Behind confident determination,

And you did seem God's son that day,
More than any of us before temptation,

But I have no doubt the desert was hot,
That days were long, nights restless,
That an empty stomach was torturous,
Making thoughts fierce and hazy,

And I think, human that I am,
That you didn't want to do it,
And given the chance you'd
Have chosen to let it pass,
And given the opportunity
It wasn't where you wished to be.

But maybe it was the morning
Of the forty-first day when
You'd grown so tired of surviving,
But you knew you'd made it
Past what you'd thought impossible

When you realized it was the truth:
That you were, that you could be,
God's son, pleasing and beloved.

For Reflection: *Recall a time when you experienced the "desert" or "wilderness" in your life. What did you learn about yourself?*

Luke 24:28–31

AS THEY came near the village to which they were going, [Jesus] walked ahead as if he were going on. But they urged him strongly, saying, "Stay with us, because it is almost evening and the day is now nearly over." So he went in to stay with them. When he was at the table with them, he took bread, blessed and broke it, and gave it to them. Then their eyes were opened, and they recognized him; and he vanished from their sight.

Upon a Smile

I was trying to pretend
I was only passing through,
That I didn't really care
If you invited me in
Or I hurried on alone.

But all I felt was lonely
As I awkwardly knocked,
Pretending nonchalance
As the door cracked open.

It had been the night
For so long.

And then when you saw me
You smiled as if
You'd been waiting for me,
As if I weren't almost a stranger,
As if I were arriving home.

And I don't remember
How I got from the stoop
To your lighted living room,
Where we talked of all
That I never knew
We had in common.

Then dinner was on the table
And a blessing offered
Over the small meal
You so willingly shared—

And you made yourself known
In the breaking of that bread.

For Reflection: *Recall a conversation or a meal when Christ was clearly present to you. What made you recognize the presence of the Lord?*

Mark 10:13–15

PEOPLE WERE bringing little children to him in order that he might touch them; and the disciples spoke sternly to them. But when Jesus saw this, he was indignant and said to them, "Let the little children come to me; do not stop them; for it is to such as these that the kingdom of God belongs."

As Your Eyes Danced

I can almost remember
The air full of the desert
And the trudging progress,
The wind scattered by indignant shouts
And the cries of merchants, buyers, sellers,
In the town you passed through that day.

With the crowds
Pressed in tightly,
And filling the street
With questions and sorrows
And laughing entreaties.

And you were talking
Where the grass mingled
With the road's dirt,
To those who were listening
And those who said they were.

The sun just kept on
Sliding across the sky,
And you were tired
And tired of the frivolous
Rhetorical games
They insisted upon.

And that was when
The little boy tottered through
The circle they'd let stand
Empty around you,
And you noticed him,
And let their questions and their tricks
Slip away,

As you knelt in the dust,
And opened your arms,
As he walked into your embrace.
You ran a gentle hand
Through the softness of his hair,
And smiled as his eyes danced with yours.

This, you told us,
Was the face
Of the kingdom of God.

Luke 2:8–10

IN THAT region there were shepherds living in the fields, keeping watch over their flock by night. Then an angel of the Lord stood before them, and the glory of the Lord shone around them, and they were terrified. But the angel said to them, "Do not be afraid; for see—I am bringing you good news of great joy for all the people."

Love, Conquering

I wonder if we've always said
That you were born at night
Because that's how it felt,

The darkness only darkening,
While loneliness crept closer
To fears we could not stifle,

Until light shone so joyously
We did not know how to feel
For the contradiction so glaring—

So much majesty and wonder
On the heels of our despair,
So much goodness to conquer evil,

As if you were so unlike us
That the world falling apart and
Hearts rent with sorrow and hate

Could only make you think
Of wholeness, of delight, of love,
Of all you longed to give us,

Wrapped, that night, in blankets,
Melting doubt and its confusion
In the purity of newborn joy.

For Reflection: *Recall a time when doubt and confusion
were changed to joy and peace. Compose a prayer of thanks-
giving for God's transforming love.*

Luke 11:5–8

AND HE said to them, "Suppose one of you has a friend, and you go to him at midnight and say to him, 'Friend, lend me three loaves of bread; for a friend of mine has arrived, and I have nothing to set before him.' And he answers from within, 'Do not bother me; the door has already been locked, and my children are with me in bed; I cannot get up and give you anything.' I tell you, even though he will not get up and give him anything because he is his friend, at least because of his persistence he will get up and give him whatever he needs."

But Secretly

And so it comes
To midnight knocking,
To you asking me to open the door
And me saying that I'm already asleep.

I'm not, of course—
I've been nibbling at my fingernails
And sipping soda distractedly,
Watching the clock click on
And waiting,
Wondering when you'd finally come.

But I don't want to let you in,
I tell myself again,
I don't want to hear
What you have to say,
I don't want to hurt
The way I hurt
When I collapse
Into your arms and sob,

Because it's so hard
To let go
Of stubbornness,
Of knowing,

It's so hard
To slide the bolt
And let you change
My "no" to "yes."

But secretly, letting you in
Is the only reason
I've stayed awake so long.

For Reflection: *What "no" in your life do you need to let Jesus change to "yes"?*

John 13:3–5

JESUS, KNOWING that the Father had given all things into his hands, and that he had come from God and was going to God, got up from the table, took off his outer robe, and tied a towel around himself. Then he poured water into a basin and began to wash the disciples' feet and to wipe them with the towel that was tied around him.

Four Months

There were tears in my eyes
From almost the moment I awoke this morning
And a desperate sort of feeling
In my heart.

My feet have been cut and bruised,
And my mind has been battered,
Partly by my own doing,
My insistence on restless nights
Of seeking for things
It's not time to find.

Partly, though, I'm stumbling
Because this is not a world
That welcomes pilgrims
Who realize this life offered
Isn't enough.

Once upon a time,
In a past that looks more like the present,
Every day,
You knelt down and washed the feet
Of a few confused men,
And I always thought I knew
What that meant.

But I've been walking now for a long time
And my feet are aching and bleeding
And when I saw you standing, waiting
Just a few steps away,
With a towel around your waist

I realized you did what you did
Partly because
You knew where you were leading
Would be hard on our feet.

For Reflection: *In what ways do you need Jesus to "wash your feet"? Compose a prayer for the openness to allow Jesus to perform this service for you.*

Mark 4:37–39

A GREAT gale arose, and the waves beat into the boat, so that the boat was already being swamped. But he was in the stern, asleep on the cushion; and they woke him up and said to him, "Teacher, do you not care that we are perishing?" He woke up and rebuked the wind, and said to the sea, "Peace! Be still!" Then the wind ceased, and there was a dead calm.

Storm's End

I've never much understood
The true masters of sleep
Who ease in and out of soporific depths,

Because if it's not bitter fought
Then it's slumber in avalanches,
Consuming an unassuming me.

So to see you there asleep
Amid no metaphorical storm,
Wind and water cascading all around,

I find myself with the disciples,
Timorously pleading you awake,
Begging for some taste of salvation.

And when at your word the storm ceased,
Marvel, we found, was no match for doubt
That raged still undeterred.

But while the others chattered,
Wondered about you among themselves,
I sat nearby as you effortlessly turned

Back to sleep and dreams you dream,
As if to say, *you just leave the storms to me.*
Sleep. We've work to do tomorrow.

For Reflection: *Call to mind a "storm" in your life that you need (or have needed) Jesus to calm. How can you (or did you) allow him to do this?*

John 6:67–69

SO JESUS asked the twelve, "Do you also wish to go away?" Simon Peter answered him, "Lord, to whom can we go? You have the words of eternal life. We have come to believe and know that you are the Holy One of God."

Left

The radio was playing
The wrong song,
And the wrong person was talking to me
About nothing.
And my eyes were overcast,
Predicting a storm to the passersby.

I let the darkness
Hide my tears.

I didn't know where else to go,
But the light was on
At the end of the alleyway,
And I slumped down
Against the dour bricks,
And trembled
Against the night,
Under your door lamp.

And when you lifted me
Off the ground and brought me in,
And threw a blanket around my shoulders,
Setting me down on your couch,
And I looked at you
Like you couldn't solve
Anything for me,
With despair
Barely hidden in my face,

You asked me
If that meant
That I was leaving, too,
That I wasn't so charmed by you
Anymore.

And I didn't have to think
Before I replied.

Where would I go,
And what would I do,
With my life
If I weren't in love with you?

And I stayed for awhile.

For Reflection: *Recall a time when you were in so much pain that it seemed that nothing could make you feel better. Where was Jesus in your pain?*

Matthew 26:6–10

NOW WHILE Jesus was at Bethany in the house of Simon the leper, a woman came to him with an alabaster jar of very costly ointment, and she poured it on his head as he sat at the table. But when the disciples saw it, they were angry and said, "Why this waste? For this ointment could have been sold for a large sum, and the money given to the poor." But Jesus, aware of this, said to them, "Why do you trouble the woman? She has performed a good service for me."

Only My Love

There was one star in the sky
As the blue drained away with the light,
And I sat muttering to myself
Grasping for some speck of meaning.

There are a thousand ways
To spend an hour other than how I have,
And had my time passed some other way
It might have been easier
To say that time hadn't been wasted.

Perhaps if I'd been thinking
Of the good things

I might open my full wallet to,
Or searching for the fruitful ways
I might put my talents to use
More perfectly,
Then I would be above question.

But tonight I could smell the ocean,
And perhaps I'm only dreaming,
But it reminded me of perfume
Bought with money someone didn't have
That could have, at least, gone to better use,
But that was, instead,
Wasted on anointing the body of a man
Who would be dead after a few sunsets,
On a cross, stinking of sweat,
And caked in his own blood.

There might have been
A thousand better ways
I could have spent the night,
But there's one star in the sky,
And I, alone as usual,
Am willing to waste
What could be put to good use
On making what little good
I know how to.

For Reflection: *Reflect on something you love to do that seems like a waste of time. Look for God in that activity.*

Mark 10:48–52

MANY STERNLY ordered [Bartimaeus] to be quiet, but he cried out even more loudly, "Son of David, have mercy on me!" Jesus stood still and said, "Call him here." And they called the blind man, saying to him, "Take heart; get up, he is calling you." So throwing off his cloak, he sprang up and came to Jesus. Then Jesus said to him, "What do you want me to do for you?" The blind man said to him, "My teacher, let me see again." Jesus said to him, "Go; your faith has made you well." Immediately he regained his sight and followed him on the way.

Past Blindness

Perhaps, actually,
He could treat epilepsy, or
It was brilliant psychotherapy:
Jesus of Nazareth, MD, PhD—

Or maybe I've tried
Too hard to understand
The incomprehensible

That Bartimaeus knew
Was nothing to be trifled with,
Nothing to let slip past
Him in his needfulness,

So he asked,
Though they said not to,
And the Lord listened
To his persistence.

And though we may explain
Sight a dozen scientific ways,
It's still God's pricking light
That illumines our eyes,

And still a flagrant faith
That sees what the Lord gives
To those willing to see
Past their blindness.

For Reflection: *Where in your life is there blindness that needs Christ's healing? How can you bring this to the Lord?*

Mark 14:43, 50—52

IMMEDIATELY, WHILE he was still speaking, Judas, one of the twelve, arrived; and with him there was a crowd with swords and clubs, from the chief priests, the scribes, and the elders....

All of them deserted him and fled. A certain young man was following him, wearing nothing but a linen cloth. They caught hold of him, but he left the linen cloth and ran off naked.

Unraveled

It was a night of unraveling:
Disciples torn apart, scattered,
Peter's faith lying in tatters,
Judas at the end of a noose,
Jesus stripped of all dignity,

And I feel like the young man,
Proud, in linen, to have stayed
When the other disciples ran,
Only to flee at a soldier's touch,
Revealed in stark vulnerability,
My outward show unraveled,
My unworthiness transparent.

And into the darkness he ran,
As Joseph finally came to light
To wrap an abandoned body
In white linen, in the love
We were afraid to give him,

Until the morning's unraveling:
Death's white shroud cast off,
Darkness unwound in light,
Hearts tied with fear unbound,

Vulnerability inwardly unraveled
To reveal the patience of faith
Not loosely wrapped in linen,
Not stitched with human hands,
But threaded through the heart of
The one who raveled the world.

For Reflection: *Recall a time when you have been stripped of dignity, or confidence, or power. Compose a prayer seeking the grace to be with Jesus in that vulnerability.*

Mark 15:33–34

WHEN IT was noon, darkness came over the whole land until three in the afternoon. At three o'clock Jesus cried out with a loud voice, "Eloi, Eloi, lema sabachthani?" which means, "My God, my God, why have you forsaken me?"

Forsaken

There was nothing
But one criminal
Dying slowly that day
For breaking the peace
With the cold metal
Weight of his words,
Feeling forsaken
By more than just the world.

And it was sin
That dripped redly down his innocent
Palms, and disbelief
That reigned in hearts
He had taught not to be lonely
Or lost anymore,

And distance that kept them,
And still keeps us, from
The foot of the cross,
As tears fall down from unforsaking
Heaven to wash his body clean,

With all creation wrapped up
In a moment that felt
Like the end of the world
But was the beginning.

Unworthiness got us
Into this thing
In the beginning,
When God created out of love
Of what was not,
And of who would kill his son,
And I weep sometimes
To know the smallest piece
Of the love held in
Slumping shoulders
And a fallen chin.

But I don't weep
For what was over,
Like death and sin,
But in sympathy for agony
I can't comprehend,

And in disbelief
And faith
At the beginning.

For Reflection: *What keeps you from standing at the foot of the cross? What draws you toward Jesus on the cross?*

Matthew 28:1—6a

AFTER THE sabbath, as the first day of the week was dawning, Mary Magdalene and the other Mary went to see the tomb. And suddenly there was a great earthquake; for an angel of the Lord, descending from heaven, came and rolled back the stone and sat on it. His appearance was like lightning, and his clothing white as snow. For fear of him the guards shook and became like dead men. But the angel said to the women, "Do not be afraid; I know that you are looking for Jesus who was crucified. He is not here; for he has been raised, as he said."

Sicut Dixit

If in the morning the letter comes
Such that you know
Before you tear the envelope,
Before you slide the letter out,
Before your eyes scan lines of type,

Still *dead* is unamusingly
A heart-stopping word,
And for all that your foreknowledge
Proves you were prepared,
You still were unready
To read it written there,

Putting life into the past tense,
Making an abstraction declarative,
Saying so simply
What you find too complex
To comprehend,

And it's love, that bewilderment,
That makes each word ache,
Such that you wish…
Except you don't wish that,
But rather that love
Could blot out death,

One word transposed
Over the other until,
Although the pain lingers,
It is love, not death,
That remains unblemished.

For Reflection: *Recall a time when Christ has transformed death into life for you, perhaps in an unexpected way.*

---

1 Corinthians 11:23–26

FOR *I* received from the Lord what I also handed on to you, that the Lord Jesus on the night when he was betrayed took a loaf of bread, and when he had given thanks, he broke it and said, "This is my body that is for you. Do this in remembrance of me." In the same way he took the cup also, after supper, saying, "This cup is the new covenant in my blood. Do this, as often as you drink it, in remembrance of me." For as often as you eat this bread and drink the cup, you proclaim the Lord's death until he comes.

Transubstantiation

I see your face in the weary,
In the worry lines, the creases below their eyes,
Their eyes that trace his fingertips
As he lifts them through the air
And says that this is the body of Christ.

And I can see the acceptance of that,
The belief before the words are even spoken,
The eager hope as he presses
The bread of life into their hands,
The confidence and unworthiness,
The years of habit and familiarity,
As they murmur "amen,"
Each in a singular way.

And I don't know
What it will be like to go home
And resume living
As any of them.
I don't know the pain,
The grief, the fear,
Or the subtle joys,
The fulfilling peace, the unending love,
Of the life behind their eyes.

But I do know
That this is the body of Christ,
Indistinguishable tonight.

For Reflection: *Recall a specific time when sharing in the celebration of the Eucharist was particularly meaningful for you. What made it meaningful and memorable?*